YOUR KNOWLEDGE HAS VALUE

Ben Messaoud

International Sales Strategy. Maketing, Sales and Distribution

GRIN Publishing

Bibliographic information published by the German National Library:

The German National Library lists this publication in the National Bibliography; detailed bibliographic data are available on the Internet at http://dnb.dnb.de .

Imprint:

Copyright © 2013 GRIN Verlag GmbH
Print and binding: Books on Demand GmbH, Norderstedt Germany
ISBN: 978-3-656-92151-6

This book at GRIN:

http://www.grin.com/en/e-book/294159/international-sales-strategy-maketing-sales-and-distribution

GRIN - Your knowledge has value

Since its foundation in 1998, GRIN has specialized in publishing academic texts by students, college teachers and other academics as e-book and printed book. The website www.grin.com is an ideal platform for presenting term papers, final papers, scientific essays, dissertations and specialist books.

Visit us on the internet:

http://www.grin.com/

http://www.facebook.com/grincom

http://www.twitter.com/grin_com

HOCHSCHULE ESSLINGEN

Fakultät Wirtschaftingenieurwesen

Hochschule Esslingen
University of Applied Sciences

Titel of Term paper-, International Sales Strategy

von: Rachid Ben Messaoud

4. Semester

Abgabetag: 22.11.2013

Contents

List of figure

Abstract

What is an international sales strategy? What about the current situation? How can I define a strategy? How do marketing and sales interact? How can a company define a sales process? What about the competition? Which tools can be used in order to optimize sales? The goal is to get an answer about all these questions. Also we should create an idea how we can companies keeping ahead of equal competitors.

1 Introduction

International Strategies and Sale are obviously two different functions in a company despite they must interact closely with each other. Exporting probably crates new markets, more sales, higher turnover and attracts new customers. That will only realize with a clear strategy. It is a fact that the global competition will increase. The European companies have to extend their international activities to stay on top in the competition with USA and Japan. The USA for example tries to get some market share in the European region and the new up coming developing Countries like the BRIC-States. Today no companies can win if its product and service resembles every other products and service of a company. Companies' products must represent a big idea in the mind of the target market.

2 General description of Strategies and Sales

2.1 Definition of Sales process

A sale is an act of selling product or service in return of money. In simple terms a sale process is a systematic approach and identification of likely customers. No matter what are a company tries to sale, mostly every sale follow the same step-by-step instruction. First, the product knowledge the Salesperson should be well informed about the product especial if it's a technical one. That will make it easily to get caught up in a dialog with a probably customer to explain all the great feature they product have. Second, prospecting is about searching new customers. The Sales department should create a customer profile, which will help to develop the appropriate marketing strategy and tactics. Third, the customers approach what is crucial for successful selling. It will tell you what your customer thinking about the products and your company. But to most import thing is to make use from these information's. Fourth, the presentation every product should be well presented especial if it's a high tech product. The last core process is close the sale after your presentation and answered all customer questions; it's now time to close the sale process. In order to succeed in sales you need to master each one of these steps. If you're weak in one or more areas, you might survive as a salesperson or company but you won't prosperity. (Kotler & Armstrong, Principles of Marketing, 2012a)

Distribution channels

A channel of distribution is the path that a product takes from producer to consumer. Nowadays distribution channels exists in varying length. A direct channel of distribution is the shortest and simplest form of distribution channel, it has become increasingly common since the advent of the Internet. Direkt distribution channel descriebes the selling act without the help of a distributor. Internet selling is one example of direct distrubution it actually describes the business to customer relation by using virtuell describition of the product like text, email or symbols.

In a indirect distrubution channel (traditional) there are as general distributors between the company and customers. A indirekt distribution channel describes no direct relation between company and customers a product will only sold in retail stores or wholesaler.

The significance of distribution channels

As mentioned, above companies requires the assistance of other distributors to reach it target market. But why do companies need the help of other to distribute their products? Is it not better to sell the products by themselves for example via Internet to earn higher profit?

Despite, there are companies such dell, which are successful without the assistance of distributers. Dell sells their products (computer) mostly, via the Internet, but in dell case they create their own transports ways to the costumers. By choosing a distribution strategy a company should think about what value the distributor should add like for example customer relation, transportation ways, customers assess and availability. Relationships in a channel (between the company and distributor) are more essential than ever.

2.2 Definition of Strategies

There are some definitions of strategies, but the most common quote is "Strategy is a high level plan to achieve one or more goals under conditions of uncertainty" or "Strategy is important because of the resources available to achieve the goals are usually limited" and "A method or plan chosen to bring about a desired future, such as achievement of a goal or solution to a problem". I want to present two additional definitions, which are more detailed. Henry Mintzberg from McGill University defines strategy as "a pattern in a stream of decisions" (Mintzberg, California Managment Review, 1987a) but he also affirms that "The field of strategy can not afford to rely on single definition of strategy, indeed the word has long been used implicitly in different ways even if it has traditionally been defined formally in only one." (Mintzberg, Management Science, 1978b) The second definition corresponding to Max McKeown implies that "strategy is about shaping the future" and the human attempt to get to "desirable ends with available means". (McKeown, 2012)

Developing the appropriate Management Strategy

The consideration of the definitions raises two questions of: first, why do we need strategies and second, what is our concern for developing strategy. Every business, regardless of the market share, property holdings and competitive environment, needs a strategy it is unusual, that a company has no competitor and is the market leader in his segment. This brings me to the point, that companies fitting in categories (like automotive or oil industry) need a plan or a strategy regardless which company it is. Strategy is crucial for keeping a company ahead of equal competitors and also to ensure key aspects for future needs.

Henry Mintzberg tries to develop strategies for all impacts. According Henry Mintzberg thinking strategically means. To start with a bridge between the past "where I'm now at the moment" and the future "where I want to be". In order to build this bridge solid, we have to follow Mintzberg's five P's of strategy. First, Plan Try to develop a plan (strategy). One example, metaphorically speaking, is a kind needs a plan to climb on a tree to pick up some apples. Accordingly a manager needs a plan to achieve his goals. At this there are a lot of models like SWOT-Analysis, Impact-Analyses, which can help you to develop, plans. Nevertheless planning by itself is not enough, that is why Mintzberg developed further four P's, such as Pattern, Ploy, Position, Perspectives. The applications of these five P's allow you to develop a robust strategy. (Mintzberg, Management Science, 1978b)

3 Marketing Environment

3.1 Domestic and International Marketing

Marketing is required by companies in order to get to know what customers want and need for being able to sell the companies products. Marketing contains planning, conception and execution of ideas, a highly educated management and at least pricing, promotion and distribution of company products. Marketing can be done within a local or domestic market or across national borders or in the international market. To ensure all these aspects, companies differentiate between Marketing in domestic and international markets. (Kotler & Armstrong, Principles of Marketing, 2012a)

Domestic Marketing

Domestic marketing involves the selling of products of a company within a local financial market. It deals with only one site of competition and economic issues, which make it more convenient to do.

There are no language barriers in a domestic market. The focus is on the local customers and market and no though is given to oversea markets. Purchasing and interpreting of data on local marketing trends and consumer demands is easier and faster to do. It helps the company making decisions and developing marketing strategies that are more effective and efficient. The risk level also decreases with domestic marketing and takes lesser financial resources. (Kotler & Armstrong, Principles of Marketing, 2012a)

International Marketing

The easiest why to describe International Marketing is that companies making one or more marketing decisions across the global. International marketing is the promotion and sale of Companies products to consumers in different countries. It is very complex and requires a huge amount of financial resources.

Michael Czinkota defined International Marketing as "[…] the marketing carried out across international borders. International marketing is a strategy that uses extension from the home country of a firm." (Czinkota, 2012) The American Marketing Association describes it "The process of planning and executing conception, pricing, promotion, and distribution of ideas, goods, and services to create exchanges that satisfy individual and organizational objectives." (Bennett, 1995)

3.2 The relationship between Sales and Marketing

Marketing and Sales may seem being disjointed, but on the highest level they share some similar goals. Firstly, both fields want to increase their turnover, selling is the highlight of a strategy generated by Marketing. According to Kotler marketing is "the science and art of exploring, creating, and delivering value to satisfy the needs of a target market at a profit. Marketing identifies unfulfilled needs and desires. It defines, measures and quantifies the size of the identified market and the profit potential. It pinpoints which segments the company is capable of serving best and it designs and promotes the appropriate products and services." (Kotler, FAQs on Marketing, 2012b) To put it simply, marketing is about increasing the desirability and value for the customer considering their wants and needs (by research), furthermore it also facilitates approaching the customer to the product, creating demand for the product and activating costumer's interest. In contrast, Sales activities are focused on converting wants and needs to the paying customers. Sales involve getting the product or service to the customer as well as Sales creates relationship and fulfilled the customer's demand. Sale is a part of marketing. Both departments are necessary for the success of a business. A company is not able to growth if one of them fails. (Kotler, FAQs on Marketing, 2012b)

4   International Sales Strategy

A sales strategy is a plan explaining how to sell products and services how to go about selling products or service or even both products and services. Nowadays, there are three basically different types of companies. First companies that make things happen, secondly those that watching things happened, thirdly the ones that wondered what happened. It is very likely that a company which "makes things happen", is based on a good Sales strategy. But is this necessary for selling products and services to be International? Why should companies go International? To answer this question we have to take a look at the global world population. The current world population is about 7.2 Billion people. From 15 to 18% (Worldometers real time world statistics, 2013) of the current world populations are living in the Industrialized countries ("North America/Australia 5,5%, Europe 11%, Japan 2%" (Worldometers real time world statistics, 2013)), and they are consuming 80% (World watch institute, 2013) of the global production. World is changing rapidly, therefore the European or American companies have to expand their international activities for creating new markets. The highly developed IT-Technology and the new infrastructure make companies able to work efficiently worldwide.

Developing countries like the "BRIC-States" will increase their incomes, jobs, improve their health care system and social-wealth, additionally the demand of products and services will rise. One the other they will try to create their own business which will raise the competition in the market. As mentioned above, a sales strategy facilitates to focus on your customer and leads the selling team (buying center) to success. All in all, every company has to develop its own sale strategy; nevertheless there are common key processes that will help to a Sale strategy.

Depiction 1: Key process

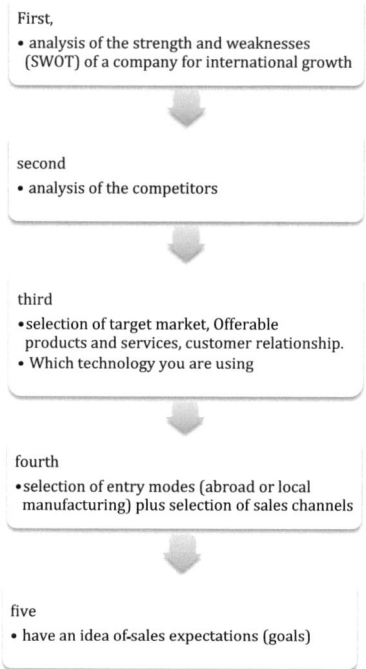

Source: (Vinci, 2013)" Strategies for Sales Perfection: In the New Economy"

Having a process idea or a document that outlines the sales strategy and sales goals will help to reach the target and achieve the goals. The Sales strategy should be aligned with the marketing strategy, which is concerned with generating and sustaining competitive advantage for the company. With the assistance of marketing, the sales strategy can focus on individual customers, interact with them and provide market segmentation. A good Sales strategy should also include

- Customer segmentation: Selection of the appropriate customer at the right time at the right place

- Customer prioritization and targeting: Prioritization of the appropriate customers and focusing on the wants and need of the customers and the market

- Use of multiple sales channels: Usage of various sale channels such as Internet selling, or "from warehouse to warehouse"

- Control the sales activities: Usage of indices to pursue the selling figures (falling sales or increasing sales numbers)

- Reaction to Competitors or Competitive situations: Adapt quickly to the fast changing market environment and situation

- Value Customer/Prospective: Understanding of customer value and offering the proper service because value is one of the key elements of selling. The information on likely selling numbers is important regarding the production of the product.

- Buying Center

- Salesperson selling process/ behaviors: Team responsible for any type of organization, it generally involves purchase decisions. (Kotler & Armstrong, Principles of Marketing, 2012a)

This paragraph will show the point "selling by setting the right price". Why the price is so substantial? Beforehand, that's the only part of the marketing mix that generates revenue; all the other 4P's actually cost money. Pricing is the process of defining what amount of money a company will obtain for its products. The company has to decide in which segment the product should be offered, for example Mercedes-Benz refers to the premium segment and on the other hand, Dacia is determined by price. There are a few ways to price a product. Price-Penetration is a price strategy basing on incredibly low prices for products and services compered to the other market competitors. After a company gains enough market shares, it slowly increases the price. This strategy is used very often in case of newly introduced magazines or shaver. Another price strategy is Price-Skimming which is a market technique allowing new products or services to be charged at the highest price a customer is willing to pay, in order to achieve maximum revenue. After the entrance of the other competitors to the market, price decreases. Parade examples are e-books sold by companies following the Price-Skimming-Strategy. (Kotler & Armstrong, Principles of Marketing, 2012a)

4.1 The International Sales Strategy by taking the example of Toyota

This passage is dedicated to the analysis of the market and the Sale Strategy by visualizing the example of Toyota. (Kotler & Armstrong, Principles of Marketing, 2012a)
Developing a good sale strategy bases on different factors. In the first place a company must overview the environment, determine the market they do operate in, identify why customers need the company? And also identify who the customers are? Beyond that it is important to answer the questions "What are we doing differently" and "Who are the competitors."
There are global players like Toyota with an aligned network of manufacturing and foundries worldwide, who operate in over 130 countries to stay on top and grow profitably. Toyota had to

adapt nimbly to the fast changing market environment. Market success grounds on solid relationship with other companies, suppliers, competitors and customers. Toyota target market is guided by the philosophy "the right car in the right place at the right time". (Toyota Motor Corporation, 2008) For instance Toyota based his target market around the globe, but also focuses especially on markets like USA, Canada, Russia, Brazil, India and the EU. According to the website Motor Trend, Toyota has in 2011 Toyota had a market share of 12,6 percent in the USA and was one of the foreign car brands market leaders in the USA, only General Motor with 19,4% and Ford with 16,5% (Lassa, 2012) had a higher market share. What is the difference between Toyota and European automobile manufacturers? The product range of Toyota starts from 10000 $ and reaches to 100000$ (Toyota, 2013), Economy class cars target on low or middle income tiers and the Luxury segment targets on middle and high income tiers. With this product variety Toyota is able to address different aged customers with various wants and needs: Toyota offers cars for sporty people and racers, but for people putting emphasis on the environment, too. So it reaches all types of customers. Toyota introduced environment-friendly cars such as a Bio-Ethanol fuel car dedicated to the Brazilian market and is still a pioneer in the hybrid-segment around the world. Further, its market strategy incorporates global, regional, and national aspects based on the assessment of customer wants and needs. Toyota places its products in the market with comfort, kindness and enthusiasm. The car company claims that its products are harmonic and emotional. Toyotas analysis grounds on the condition of the market, economy and purchasing capacity of the costumer. Relating to these facts, Toyota is a company that makes things happen. (Kotler & Armstrong, Principles of Marketing, 2012a)

This shows the vehicle service satisfaction in Australia:

Depiction 2: Customer satisfaction

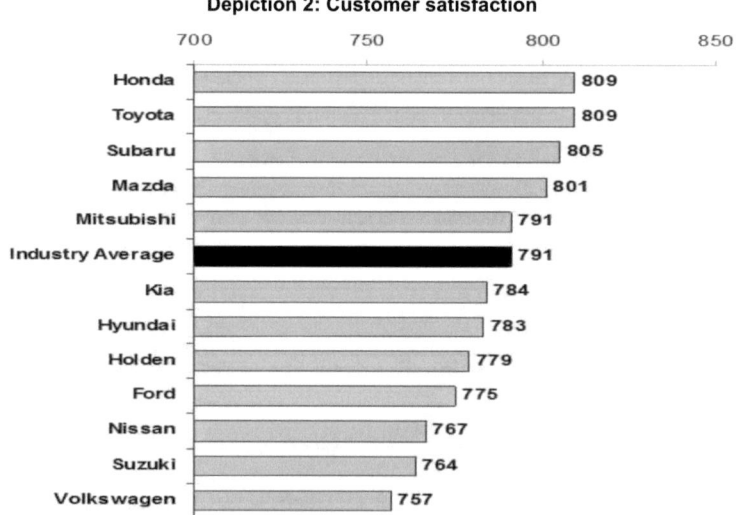

Source: (Zalstein, 2012) "Toyota, Honda top Australian vehicle service satisfaction survey" Car advice

4.2 Conclusion and Summary

Sale is a key element to the company because their position is the point of contact with the market. Everything depends on their ability to find and uncover needs to solve customer problems to transmit the right sales story and in general to achieve the highest level of professionalism. Also there is a special relationship between sales and marketing a company will not be able to sale their product without a good marketing strategy. All in all I can say that sales and strategies must interact closely to achieve the goals of the company.

5 List of literature

Zalstein, D. (2012). Toyota, Honda top Australian vehicle service satisfaction survey. *Car adivice* .

Vinci, T. (2013). *Strategies for Sales Perfection: In the New Economy.* Uk: CreateSpace Independent Publishing Platform.

Bennett, P. D. (1995). *Dictionary of Marketing Terms.* US: American Marketing Association.

Czinkota, M. (2012). *International Marketing.* US.

Kotler, P. (2012b). *FAQs on Marketing.*

Kotler, P., & Armstrong, G. (2012a). *Principles of Marketing.*

Krishnaswamy, S., Kotler, P., & Rackham, N. (2006). Ending the War Between Sales and Marketing. *Havard Business Review* .

Lassa, T. (2012). *U.S Market Share for the Top Five Automarks.* US: Motor Trend.

Mintzberg, H. (1987a). *California Management Review.* CA.

Mintzberg, H. (1978b). *Management Science.* CA.

The Global Marketing Network. (n.d.). Retrieved from http://www.gmnhome.com/

Toyota Motor Corporation. (2008). *Driving to innovate.* Tokio: Toyota Motor Corporation.

Toyota. (2013). *Toyota.* Retrieved from www.toyota.com